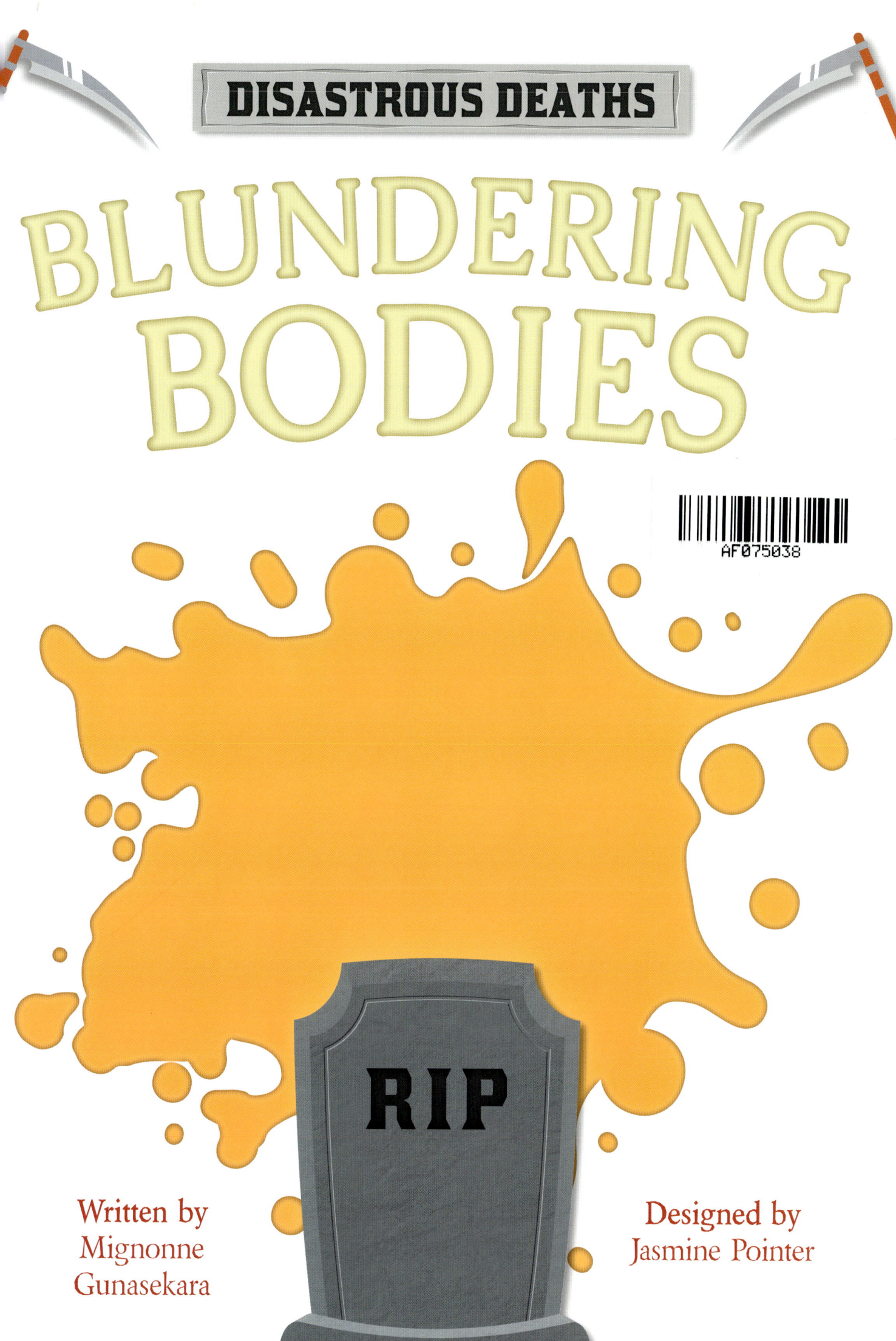

DISASTROUS DEATHS

BLUNDERING BODIES

Written by
Mignonne
Gunasekara

Designed by
Jasmine Pointer

All rights reserved.
Printed in Malaysia.

A catalogue record for this book is available from the British Library.

ISBN: 978-1-83927-816-7

Written by:
Mignonne Gunasekara

Edited by:
John Wood

Designed by:
Jasmine Pointer

All facts, statistics, web addresses and URLs in this book were verified as valid and accurate at time of writing. No responsibility for any changes to external websites or references can be accepted by either the author or publisher.

©2020
BookLife Publishing Ltd.
King's Lynn
Norfolk PE30 4LS

PHOTO CREDITS

All images are courtesy of Shutterstock.com, unless otherwise specified. With thanks to Getty Images, Thinkstock Photo and iStockphoto. Background texture throughout – Abstracto. Gravestone throughout – MaryValery. Front Cover – Panda Vector, Taleseedum. 5 – Graphic Treasure, Praisaeng. 7 – Marko Poplasen. 8 – Giuseppe Porta [Public domain], Tim UR. 9 – British Museum [Public domain], romawka, ONYXprj. 11 – ONYXprj, Valentin Agapov. 12 – https://commons.wikimedia.org/wiki/File:Hans_Staininger.jpg, Mathew Brady [Public domain], Paper Teo, Christophe BOISSON, Migren Art, Alfmaler. 13 – Olga Popova, Roger Higgins, World Telegram staff photographer [Public domain], ONYXprj. 14 – Antonov Maxim, Uncimo. 15 – guteksk7. 16 – Frederico Moeller, Eduard Ender (1822-1883) [Public domain], StockVector. 17 – SvetlanaSF, lynea, Colorcocktail, mStudioVector. 18 – ONYXprj. 19 – bioraven, Nora Hachio. 20 – Everett Historical, Hong Vo, ONYXprj, Oceloti, ImLucky. 21 – Alan Kelly, oranoot, KittyVector, Anna.zabella. 22 – Macrovector. 23 – NataliaVo. 24 – Mick Atkins, VectorArtFactory. 25 – gabriel12. 27 – artbesouro, Mountain Brothers. 28 – unknown, after Francis Cotes (1726-1770) [Public domain], Super8, Waeel quttene, SilviaC. 29 – donsimon, National Portrait Gallery [Public domain]*, Elegant Solution, Vector Plotnikoff, Morphart Creation. * – U.S. work public domain in the U.S. for unspecified reason but presumably because it was published in the U.S. before 1924.
Additional illustrations by Jasmine Pointer.

CONTENTS

Page 4	Welcome to the Disaster Zone
Page 6	Chrysippus of Soli
Page 8	What's So Funny?
Page 10	Hans Steininger
Page 12	Hairy Business
Page 14	Tycho Brahe
Page 16	Mind Your Manners
Page 18	Sir Francis Bacon
Page 20	Snow Way to Go
Page 22	Frank Hayes
Page 24	You Win Some, You Lose Some
Page 26	Maria Gunning
Page 28	Beauty Is Pain
Page 30	Timeline of Death
Page 31	Glossary
Page 32	Index

Words that look like this are explained in the glossary on page 31.

WELCOME TO THE DISASTER ZONE

History is full of grisly stories and weird tales... and a lot of death. From the battlefield to the home, from rich royals to those who didn't have much money at all, people in the past got up to some pretty strange stuff during their lives. So it makes perfect sense for some of those people's lives to have ended in ways that were just as strange.

Around seven percent of all the people who have ever lived are alive right now. How cool is that? You know what that means... there are loads of deaths to choose from!

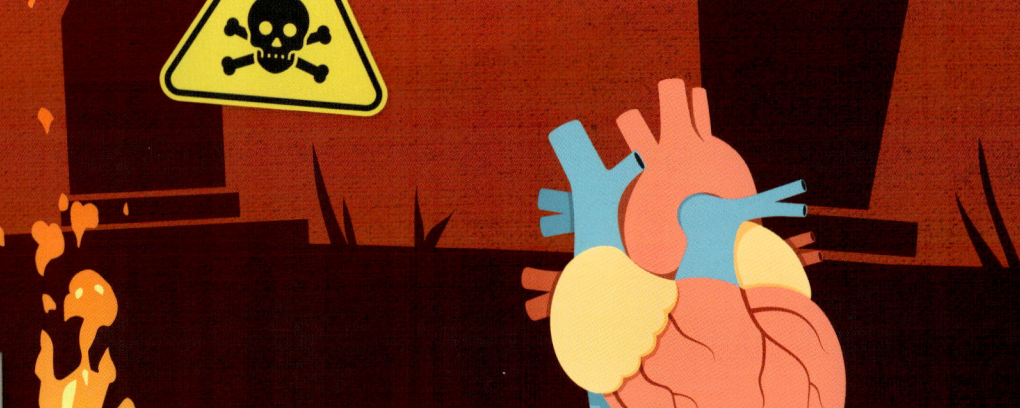

In this book, we are going to look at the stories of six people who were taken out by their own blundering bodies. Whether they did something they shouldn't have or whether it was a complete surprise, we'll find out about the many bizarre ways in which these unfortunate people met their disastrous ends.

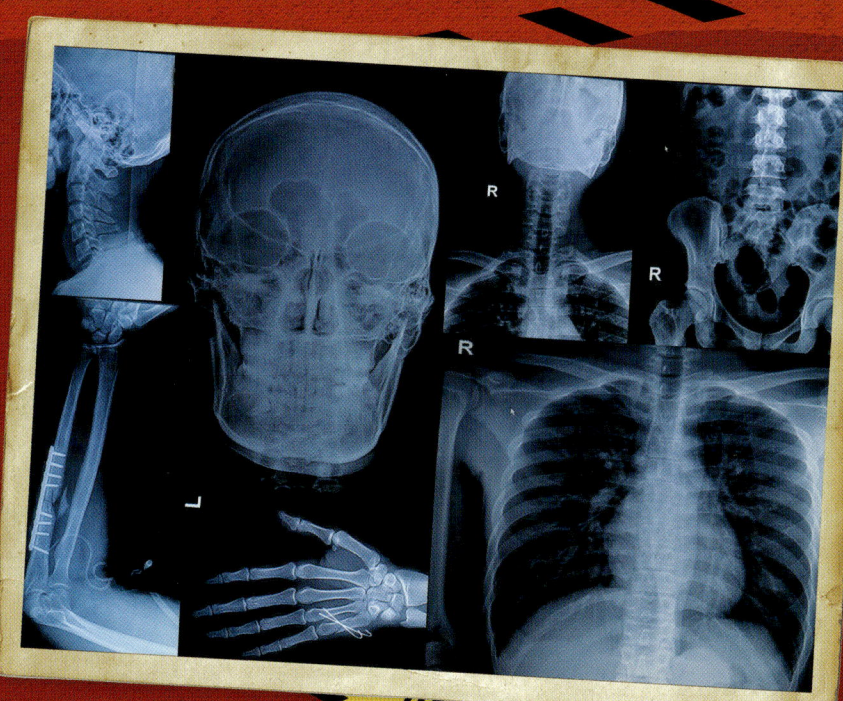

INTO THE DISASTER ZONE WE GO...

Throughout history, there have been lots of names and sayings that mean someone has died.

Here are a few of the weird ones:

Snuffed
Bit the dust
The big sleep
Six feet under
Counting worms
Pushing up daisies

CHRYSIPPUS OF SOLI

Chrysippus was an ancient Greek <u>philosopher</u>. He was born in Soli, an area that is now part of Turkey. He ended up moving to Athens. There, he became a student of Cleanthes, who was the head of a school of philosophy. When Cleanthes died, Chrysippus took over as head of the school. Chrysippus ended up becoming quite a big deal for his philosophy.

There are many stories about Chrysippus' death. One of the more interesting ones says that he saw a donkey eating figs, and cracked a joke that someone should give the donkey wine. He thought this was all so funny that he laughed himself to death.

Philosophy is the study of life. It involves asking questions about how people should live their lives.

WHAT'S SO FUNNY?

If this story about Chrysippus' death is true, it would be very ironic because he was a Stoic philosopher. Stoic philosophers study Stoicism, which is a type of philosophy from ancient Greece. This philosophy says self-control and strength are important in order to be calm and get over bad emotions. If you are calm, you can make better choices.

A drawing of Chrysippus laughing at the donkey

For the Stoic philosophers, self-control was very important. Chrysippus must have found that donkey really funny if he lost control and laughed like that.

Figs

Stoic philosophers believed that the way to make good choices and live a good life was by using logic.

Chrysippus' Contribution

Chrysippus is thought of as a very important philosopher in Stoicism. He wrote over 700 pieces of work about the subject. Sadly, none of those pieces of work are around today, but parts of them are included in the writing of philosophers that came after Chrysippus.

Hey, a donkey's got to eat.

Chrysippus of Soli

Chrysippus spent a lot of time on his ideas – people say that he wrote at least 500 lines of work a day. He loved debating and he especially liked looking at both sides of arguments.

The only problem was that Chrysippus liked to argue both sides of an idea himself, at the same time!

HANS STEININGER

Hans Steininger was the mayor of Braunau am Inn, Austria, during the 16th century. He was well liked by the people of the town, who <u>voted</u> to keep him as mayor several times.

Hans was famous for his incredibly long beard, which was around two metres long! To keep it out of the way, Hans would bundle his beard up into a pouch or pocket. Sadly, during a horrible fire in 1567, Hans died when he tripped over his beard and fell down some stairs. He hadn't had a chance to tuck his beard out of the way in the panic the fire had caused. To keep the memory of Hans alive, the townspeople put up statues of him.

In addition to the statues, Hans' beard was put on display in Braunau's District Museum. You can still go to see it today.

HAIRY BUSINESS

Hans is not the only person in history to have had such famous facial hair. Let's take a look at a few others:

Ambrose Burnside

Ambrose Burnside was a general during the American Civil War. He set the trend for this now-famous style of facial hair called sideburns, which is named after him and his wondrous whiskers. Ambrose was not especially successful in his military career, but he was successful at having amazing sideburns. What a way to be remembered.

Hans Steininger

Ambrose Burnside, 1824–1881

Hair grows, on average, around 1.25 centimetres a month – the only other part of the human body that grows faster than that is bone marrow.

12

Edward Teach

'Blackbeard', 1680–1718

EDWARD TEACH (BLACKBEARD) AND PIRATE KETCH

Edward Teach is probably better known by another name – 'Blackbeard'. This famous pirate roamed the southeast US and the Caribbean during the early 18th century, capturing ships and stealing treasure. He is said to have worn his beard in dreadlocks, with slow-burning fuses wound into it. Before a fight, Edward would light the fuses so that smoke billowed from his beard. Imagine having facial hair that is so cool you can use it as your name.

Salvador Dalí

Salvador Dalí was a Spanish artist. He painted very strange but interesting paintings. He was also a strange but interesting person, with a very unusual moustache.

Salvador Dalí, 1904–1989

Salvador Dalí's body was dug up in 2017, and his moustache was still perfectly styled.

TYCHO BRAHE

Tycho Brahe was a Danish <u>astronomer</u> and a man of manners. He was an important person in astronomy as we know it today. Over the years, he made notes on over 1,000 new stars! There is even a crater on the Moon named after him.

The story of Tycho's death tells us that he was at a banquet when he needed a wee. In those days, however, people thought that getting up in the middle of a meal was rude. So, polite Tycho held his wee in and kept eating and drinking. This was a big mistake. Holding his wee in like that did something bad to his kidneys or bladder. Tycho became very ill and was dead just 11 days later.

Some people thought that Tycho was actually poisoned to death with mercury, but experts now think this was not true.

MIND YOUR MANNERS

Murder Most Foul

Tycho Brahe

If Tycho had been poisoned, who would have wanted him out of the way? Some scientists thought that Johannes Kepler could have wanted to poison Tycho. Johannes was another astronomer who went on to become quite famous himself. At the time, he lived with Tycho as an assistant, so Johannes definitely had the chance to poison him.

'Tycho' is a crater on the Moon

Others argue that this made no sense. Tycho was trying to get Johannes a job working for the emperor at the time. Why would Johannes do something that would ruin his chance at such a good job?

In 1566, Tycho lost part of his nose in a sword fight and had to wear a metal prosthetic for the rest of his life.

Funny about Forks

Good table manners as we know them today are quite new ideas. People only used knives to eat for the most part, and they wiped their hands on the tablecloth instead of napkins!

A table fit for a banquet

In 1533, Catherine de Medici married the future king of France, Henry II. Catherine had grown up in Italy, but moved to France after her marriage. She was used to eating with a fork in Italy, but many people in France laughed at her. They did not use forks, but ate with knives or their hands instead.

Catherine de Medici

People in those days may not have liked forks because they look like the devil's pitchfork and share a similar name.

SIR FRANCIS BACON

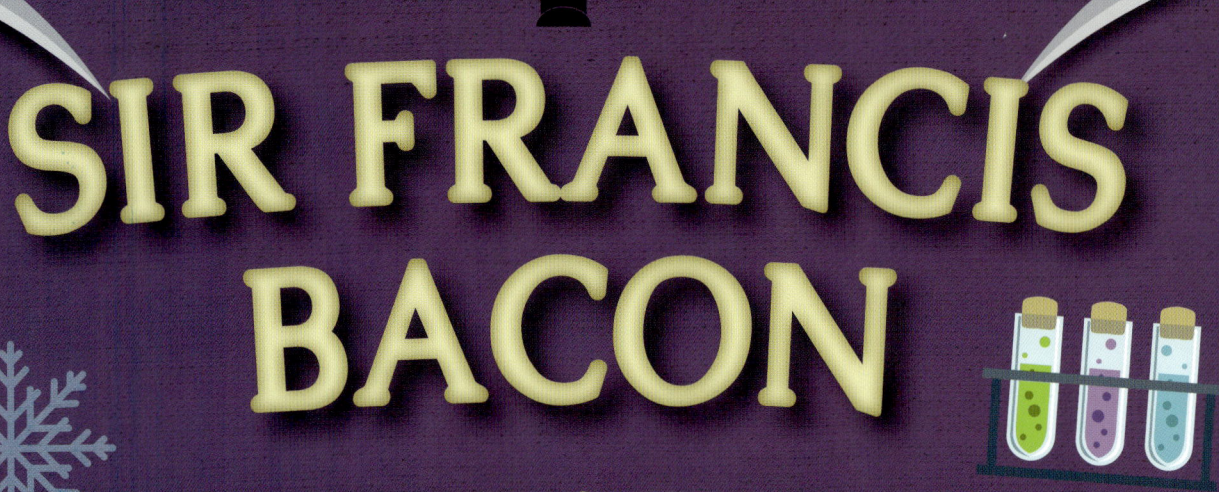

Sir Francis Bacon was a man of many talents. He had lots of important jobs and interesting hobbies, including the study of philosophy and science. He was always thinking of new ideas that he could work on.

One of those ideas came to him on a cold winter's day when he was taking a carriage ride through London. Sir Francis thought that snow may be able to keep uncooked meat fresh for a while, like salt did. He stopped the carriage and bought an uncooked chicken from a woman in Highgate Hill. He stuffed the chicken full of snow to see if his idea was correct. Handling the cold snow apparently made Sir Francis very ill, and he died not long afterwards.

Some say the ghost of the chicken that Sir Francis stuffed with snow still roams around Highgate, squawking and flapping its wings.

BORN: London, England
DIED: London, England
CLAIM TO FAME: Being really clever
DEATH BY: Frozen chicken

This will be worth it!

1561–1626

SNOW WAY TO GO

Sir Francis was onto something – low temperatures do keep food fresher for longer. That's why most homes today have fridges and freezers to store food in. But how did people keep their food from spoiling or rotting before fridges and freezers were available?

Sir Francis Bacon

Keepin' It Fresh

It is thought that the ancient Egyptians and other cultures across the Middle East and Asia used wind and the warm sunlight to dry their food. This went as far back as 12,000 BC. Meat, fruit and vegetables can all be dried and then stored until needed.

Beef jerky is made by drying pieces of beef. It doesn't need to be kept in the fridge.

Frozen fish

People that lived in cold parts of the world used the snow and ice there to their advantage. They could bury meat in the snow or underground and it would act like a freezer.

Brr-illiant Birdseye

Clarence Birdseye caused a stir in the frozen food industry with his method of 'quick freezing'. Clarence had seen the Inuit people of Canada freezing fish as soon as they were caught. The fish still tasted fresh when it was cooked much later, and Clarence realised this was because of how quickly it had been frozen.

The door to an old ice cellar

People used ice cellars or ice houses, which were cold underground rooms, for keeping ice and food stored on ice.

FRANK HAYES

In the summer of 1923, Frank Hayes won first place in a horse race at Belmont Park in New York. He was normally a horse trainer rather than a jockey, and this was the first time he'd ever won a race. He rode a horse called Sweet Kiss, and together they crossed the finish line way ahead of all the other racers. When people gathered around Frank to congratulate him after the race, they got a nasty surprise. Frank was dead.

Frank had died from a heart attack during the race, but he somehow didn't fall out of the saddle. Stress and losing weight for the race in a short amount of time probably caused Frank's heart attack.

Rumour has it that after this deadly race, Sweet Kiss became known as Sweet Kiss of Death.

YOU WIN SOME, YOU LOSE SOME

Horse races seem to be very eventful. Let's take a look at a couple more interesting stories that have come out of the races:

Equine Imposter

In 1844, the winner of the Epsom Derby was <u>disqualified</u> for cheating. The oldest a horse was allowed to be to compete in the race was three years old, but the winner was actually four years old. The horse, named Maccabeus, was made to look like another horse called Running Rein by having its hair dyed. Maccabeus sneakily took Running Rein's place in the race at the very last minute.

Even being one year older makes a horse bigger and stronger and therefore more likely to win the race.

Never Mind, Take Two

A steeplechase in 1945 saw a record set... for the slowest time ever taken to win such a race. A horse named Never Mind II had refused to jump over a fence quite early on, so his rider had given up and left the racetrack.

A racehorse and jockey jumping over a hurdle during a race

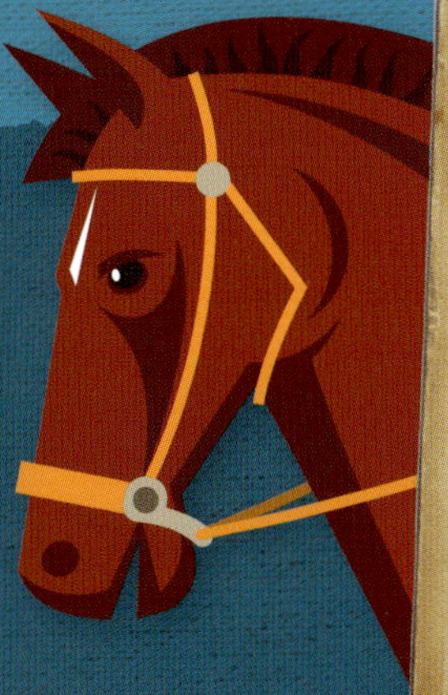

Never Mind II's rider then heard that all the other horses in the race had been disqualified or had not made it to the finish line. The two of them returned to the track and ended up winning with a time of 11 minutes and 28 seconds.

A steeplechase is a race where runners or horses have to leap over hurdles, such as hedges, along the way.

MARIA GUNNING

Maria Gunning grew up in Ireland and eventually became an actress. As Maria's fame increased, she moved to London, where everyone thought she was drop-dead gorgeous. Maria was now a celebrity with countless fans that waited by the stage door for her every time she performed. Her life was going well, but something was eating away at Maria – quite literally.

The makeup she wore everyday was turning to acid and melting the skin off her face. This only made her apply more makeup to try to cover up the scars. She used products that contained lead and mercury, which are both very harmful. She is thought to have died of poisoning brought on by the makeup she used.

Maria's fans were obsessed with her. She needed guards to go with her and keep her safe when she went for walks.

BEAUTY IS PAIN

In Maria Gunning's day, white skin and rosy cheeks were thought to be very beautiful. If you wanted to make your skin whiter and your cheeks rosier, there were products you could buy to help.

Maria used something called 'Venetian ceruse' to whiten her skin. It was made with lead, which is poisonous. She applied cinnabar to her cheeks, but this was made with mercury, which is also poisonous. The red lipstick Maria used was also made with mercury. In large amounts like this, lead and mercury are deadly.

Maria Gunning

An ancient eyeliner pot

An antique powder box

Wearing these makeup products every day meant the lead and mercury could seep past Maria's skin and get into her blood.

Maybe She's Born with It, Maybe It's Lead Poisoning

Maria was only following the lead of those before her. Ancient Greek and Roman women also used to whiten their faces with lead-based makeup. Ancient Egyptian eyeliner, worn by both men and women as 'protection' from sunlight and illness, was made using lead as well.

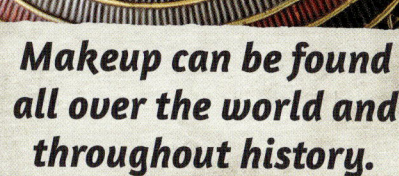

Makeup can be found all over the world and throughout history.

Lead would make a person's skin change colour, hair fall out and their teeth crumble. This is what is said to have happened to Elizabeth I who, like Maria, loved to use Venetian ceruse.

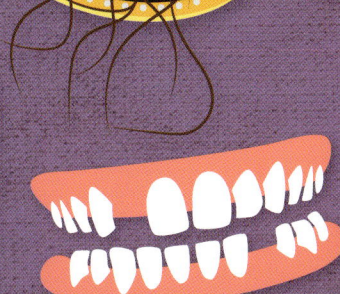

Queen Elizabeth I wanted to cover up her smallpox scars with makeup.

TIMELINE OF DEATH

Chrysippus
207 BC

Hans Steininger
1567

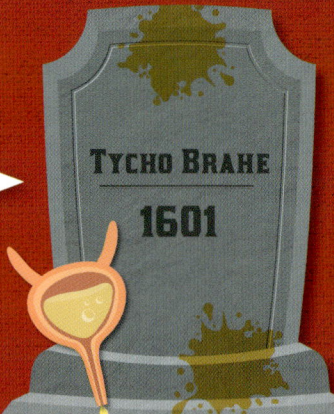

Tycho Brahe
1601

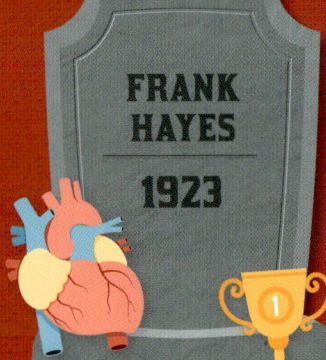

Frank Hayes
1923

Maria Gunning
1760

Sir Francis Bacon
1626

GLOSSARY

AMERICAN CIVIL WAR — a war between different groups in the US that took place from 1861–1865

ASTRONOMER — a person who studies the universe and objects in space

AVERAGE — the typical amount or most central number of a range of numbers

BC — meaning 'before Christ', it is used to mark dates that occurred before the starting year of most calendars

BONE MARROW — spongy tissue found inside some bones in the body, including the hip and thigh bones

DEBATING — having a formal or serious discussion about a topic

DISQUALIFIED — not counted because of something done that was against the rules

DREADLOCKS — a hairstyle that involves twisting the hair into thick strands

FUSES — pieces of rope or other materials that have been soaked in something that can be lit on fire

IRONIC — to happen in a way that is typically opposite to what would be expected

LOGIC — the science of using careful thought to make decisions

PHILOSOPHER — a person who studies the nature of knowledge, reality and existence

POSTHUMOUS — happening after death

PROSTHETIC — relating to a human-made body part that is often used to replace a natural one that has been lost or damaged

VOTED — expressed a choice or opinion, often through writing a mark on a piece of paper

INDEX

A
ancient Egyptians 20, 29

B
beards 10–11, 13

D
debates 9
donkeys 6–9

F
fires 10
food 6–8, 14, 18–21
forks 17

G
Greece 6–8

H
horses 22–25

K
Kepler, Johannes 16

L
laughter 6–8, 17
leaders 17, 29

M
makeup 26–29
manners 14, 17
mercury 14, 26, 28
moustaches 13

P
philosophy 6–9, 18
pirates 13

R
racing 22–25

S
snow 18, 21